SAE EDGE™
RESEARCH REPORT

Unsettled Technology Domains in Industrial Metrology

Dr. Jody E. Muelaner
Muelaner Engineering Ltd.

CONTRIBUTORS

Patrick Keogh, *University of Bath*
Glen Mullineux, *University of Bath*
Nenad Sarcevic, *Airbus Operations Ltd.*
Peter Marchbank, *Rotary Precision Instruments*
Ian Whitehead, *Rotary Precision Instruments*
Andrew Portsmore, *GKN Aerospace*

SAE INTERNATIONAL®
Warrendale, Pennsylvania, USA

About the Publisher

SAE International® is a global association of more than 128,000 engineers and related technical experts in the aerospace, automotive, and commercial-vehicle industries. Our core competencies are lifelong learning and voluntary consensus standards development. Visit sae.org.

SAE EDGE™ Research Report Disclaimer

SAE EDGE™ Research Reports focus on topics that are dynamic, in which knowledge is incomplete, and which have yet to be standardized. They represent the collective wisdom of a group of experts and serve as a practical guide to the reader in understanding unsettled subject matter. They are not meant to provide a recommended practice or protocol. The experts engaged have contributed their own thoughts and points of view, and these are not the positions of the institutions or businesses with which they are affiliated. A professional writer has collectivized their input; there is no one contributor's perspective being advanced but rather that of a community of practitioners. SAE EDGE™ Research Reports are the property of SAE International, and SAE alone is responsible for their content.

About This Publication

SAE EDGE™ Research Reports provide state-of-the-art and state-of-industry examinations of the most significant topics in mobility engineering. SAE EDGE™ contributors are experts from research, academia, and industry who have come together to explore and define the most critical advancements, challenges, and future direction in areas such as vehicle automation, unmanned aircraft, IoT and connectivity, cybersecurity, advanced propulsion, and advanced manufacturing.

Related Resources

SAE MOBILUS® Advanced Manufacturing Knowledge Hub
https://saemobilus.sae.org/advanced-manufacturing/

SAE Team

Frank Menchaca, Chief Product Officer
Michael Thompson, Director, Standards, Information and Research Publications
Courtney Howard, Editorial Director
Monica Nogueira, Acquisitions Director
Jill Leonard, Product Manager
William Kucinski, Managing Technical Editor

Printed in USA

ISSN 2640-3536
eISSN 2640-3544
ISBN 978-1-4686-0104-6

To purchase bulk quantities, please contact: SAE Customer Service

E-mail: CustomerService@sae.org
Phone: 877-606-7323 (*inside USA and Canada*)
724-776-4970 (*outside USA*)
Fax: 724-776-0790

Visit the SAE International Bookstore at books.sae.org

About the Editor

Dr. Jody E. Muelaner is a chartered mechanical engineer with a background in metrology, aerospace manufacturing, and machine design. He now specializes in writing about technical topics in a way that the target audience can easily understand.

His writing has included technical reports for Rolls-Royce and Airbus, peer-reviewed journals, and UK Government reports, as well as magazines and websites. He has published several hundred articles and was awarded the Sage Best Paper Award in 2010.

Starting out in machine design, Dr. Muelaner initially worked on sawmills, waste processing machinery, domestic appliances, and medical devices. After moving into metrology, his research focused on modeling and optimizing uncertainty in manufacturing systems, enabling right-the-first-time assembly, and the design of innovative laser instruments. He founded Muelaner Engineering Ltd in 2018 to provide consultancy and technical writing within advanced manufacturing and machine design.

contents

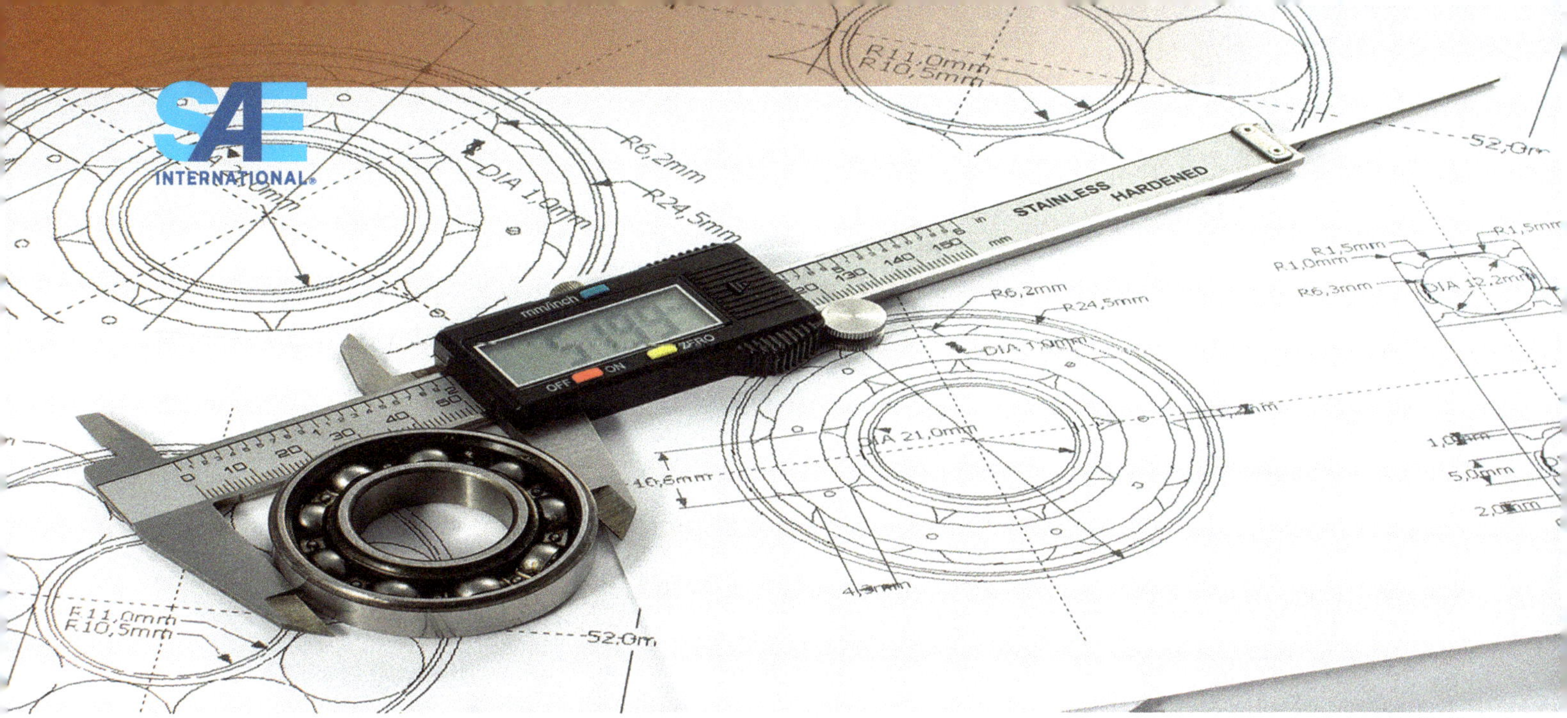

Audrius Merfeldas/Shutterstock.com

Unsettled Technology Domains in Industrial Metrology

Abstract

Within manufacturing, measurements are used to make decisions related to product verification and process control. The selection of production machines and instruments involves a trade-off to achieve the required accuracy while minimizing cost. Similarly, deciding on the level of confidence at which products are rejected is a trade-off between the cost of rejecting acceptable parts and the cost of passing substandard products to the customer. These trade-offs can only be optimized if the uncertainties are fully understood. Currently multiple methodologies are used to understand uncertainties and variation within manufacturing, such as measurement systems analysis (MSA), statistical process control (SPC), and uncertainty evaluation. The industry lacks a unified approach that provides a complete understanding of uncertainty. This means that optimal decisions cannot be made to maximize the profitability of production systems.

NOTE: SAE EDGE™ Research Reports are intended to identify and illuminate key issues in emerging, but still unsettled, technologies of interest to the mobility industry. The goal of SAE EDGE™ Research Reports is to stimulate discussion and work in the hope of promoting and speeding resolution of identified issues. SAE EDGE™ Research Reports are not intended to resolve the issues they identify or close any topic to further scrutiny.

DR. JODY E. MUELANER

Muelaner Engineering Ltd.

Contributors

Patrick Keogh, *Professor, University of Bath*
Glen Mullineux, *University of Bath*
Nenad Sarcevic, *Metrologist and Process Engineer, Airbus Operations Ltd.*
Peter Marchbank, *Chief Executive Officer, Rotary Precision Instruments*
Ian Whitehead, *Technical Manager, Rotary Precision Instruments*
Andrew Portsmore, *Technology Manager, Assembly and Inspection, GKN Aerospace*

ISSN 2640-3536

Introduction

State of the Industry

Within manufacturing, measurements are used to make decisions related to product verification and process control. Manufacturers must ensure that components fit together during assembly and that the final product meets the required specifications for form, fit, and function. It requires a certain level of accuracy in production processes and measurements. The selection of production machines and instruments involves a trade-off to achieve the required accuracy while minimizing cost. Similarly, deciding on the level of confidence at which products are rejected is a trade-off between the cost of rejecting acceptable parts and the cost of passing substandard products to the customer. For example, an aircraft which does not meet tolerance requirements for its wing profile has reduced aerodynamic efficiency and a concession is given to the customer. In 2017, Airbus lost £6.6 billion in sales revenue to concessions [1].

Production system profitability depends on trade-offs which can only be optimized if the uncertainties of measurements are fully understood. Measurement is sometimes seen as a means to improve quality and sometimes as an unnecessary cost. A methodology of selecting production and inspection processes that maximizes profit is required to make rational decisions. Such an approach depends on an understanding of uncertainties so that the probability of different cost implications can be accounted for; it can also be considered as a means of quantifying risks.

Developments such as non-contact sensors and the Internet of Things mean that the volume of available measurement data is increasing rapidly. The move to increasingly flexible production systems simultaneously means a greater reliance on metrology data. Our understanding of the uncertainty of this data has not, however, kept up with these developments and in many cases has declined as contact measurements have been replaced by non-contact measurements [2]. The industry is, therefore, confronted with large quantities of data from which it is not possible to draw statistically valid conclusions.

Manufacturing decisions involving measurement typically answer one of five generic questions:

Product verification questions

1. Is an instrument capable of proving product conformance?
2. Does a measurement result give sufficient confidence to accept or reject a part

Process control questions

3. Is an instrument capable of providing meaningful data about a particular process?
4. Is a production process capable of producing a conforming product?
5. Is a production process changing in a way that indicates it will soon not be capable?

Questions 1 and 3 may also be rephrased as "What would the most appropriate instrument be for this measurement task?" The capability of measurements to verify products and monitor processes is typically evaluated using an measurement systems analysis (MSA) approach. It means using gauge studies in which references are measured repeatedly and statistical analysis is used to determine the accuracy of the measurement system. Such an approach usually cannot, for practical reasons, consider all sources of uncertainty. It can cause overconfidence in measurement results with subsequent issues for product quality and production system efficiency. Widespread interest exists within the industry in applying more rigorous methods of uncertainty evaluation to these industrial measurements; however, there is currently no general agreement about how this could be achieved and there are some fundamental issues with doing so.

Where quality issues are detected, inspection processes must also ensure that sufficient data has been obtained to support subsequent root cause analysis. Measurement has an important diagnostic role to play.

The issues fall into the following unresolved domains:

- **A comprehensive uncertainty framework for industrial measurement** is needed to provide a consistent language and methodology which will enable system-wide considerations of the production system to utilize uncertainty information. Currently different terminology and methods are used for equivalent functions within three methodologies: metrology, MSA, and statistical process control (SPC).
- **Evaluation of Type B uncertainties** in industrial measurements is required to enable the consideration of effects that haven't been directly observed, such as calibration uncertainty.
- **Evaluating intrinsic uncertainty**: A finite number of discrete measurements, even if the measurements have no uncertainty, leave uncertainty about the unmeasured regions. There are no established methods of quantifying this uncertainty.
- **Evaluate the expected uncertainty** for measurement processes. Current uncertainty evaluation methods only apply to individual measurements after they have been carried out. Manufacturing decisions often require before-the-fact evaluation for processes.
- **Standard industrial uncertainty models**, which allow shared models for instrument and machine elements, and environmental effects will enable complex systems to be readily modeled.
- **Verifying industrial uncertainty models** gives confidence that models are correct.
- **Summarize and extrapolate from Monte Carlo simulation (MCS)** such that complex simulation results can be communicated, and optimization can consider the probability of rare events.

If all sources of uncertainty in industrial measurement processes are understood, then it will greatly enhance decisions within manufacturing. It will be possible to state, with statistical confidence, whether a product conforms to a specification. However, this factor alone will not enable measurement data to inform optimal trade-offs in manufacturing. For example, when selecting instruments for product conformance, it is possible to determine expected false pass and false rejection rates for each instrument; however, to make optimal trade-offs, instruments and processes must be selected for maximum profit, taking into account costs associated with false decision rates. Currently, methods of determining capability within MSA simply aim to achieve arbitrary targets [3] which cannot be optimal for all products and processes. These considerations lead to two additional unresolved domains:

- **Making optimal product verification decisions** involving the selection of instruments, processes, and conformance limits
- **Making optimal process control decisions** involving the selection of instruments, processes, and conformance limits

The vision is a future production system which makes optimal trade-offs between cost and quality. It will select production machines and inspection instruments, recalibrate instruments and machines in real time, and determine when to reject or rework products. It will be enabled by robust techniques for evaluating uncertainty in production, inspection, and calibration, both during planning and in-process. These uncertainties will be used to calculate conditional probabilities for outcomes such as a defective product reaching the customer. In turn, these probabilities will enable cost-based optimization algorithms to configure and operate the production system.

Beyond resolving the technical issues, comprehensive education in metrology will be required. Undergraduate-level engineering studies currently provide very little metrology curriculum. An approach to optimizing production systems that is founded on uncertainty will require a much higher level of education in this field.

A Comprehensive Uncertainty Framework for Industrial Measurement

Domains concerning specific sources of uncertainty have been identified in the introduction, and each is discussed in detail in the following sections, for example, evaluating intrinsic and expected uncertainties. This section will not duplicate discussion of these domains. However, it is important that they are not addressed in isolation from each other. A comprehensive framework is required to provide a consistent language and methodology. A consistent representation of uncertainty will enable system-wide considerations of the production system.

Within the industry, uncertainty evaluation, following the "Evaluation of measurement data - Guide to the expression of uncertainty in measurement" (GUM) [4], is primarily used for laboratory-based calibrations of instruments such as gauge blocks and micrometers [5] which are calibrated with stated *uncertainties*. Newer and more complex instruments, such as coordinate measurement machines (CMMs) [6] and laser trackers [7], are often verified to give a *maximum permissible error* (MPE) without providing full uncertainty statements. Within the production environment, measurement processes are generally evaluated using MSA, as recommended in Six Sigma [8]. MSA involves *gauge study* [9]. Process outputs are kept under *statistical control* using control charts to identify *common cause* and *special cause variation*, according to the SPC methodology [10].

The methods share common principles related to errors, accuracy, and uncertainty, but they define terms differently. The way they consider systemic effects also has some differences with only the GUM providing a rigorous approach, discussed in greater depth in the following section on **Evaluating Type B Uncertainties**.

The following subsections describe some generic themes shared by the GUM, MSA, and SPC. The differences in language and methodology are discussed, as well as commonalities.

Error, Accuracy, and Uncertainty

An *error* of measurement is the difference between the result of a measurement and the true value of the measurand. Error is sometimes confused with uncertainty, but that refers to a completely different concept. If a measurement is repeated, then the true value will remain the same, but each result will be different due to each measurement including different errors. It is not possible to know the true value or the error exactly. However, it is possible to estimate how close the true value is likely to be to the measurement result. This is the quantity expressed as accuracy or uncertainty. It may be noted that, within the *International Vocabulary of Metrology - Basic and General Concepts and Associated Terms* (VIM) [11], accuracy is not to be used quantitatively, but within MSA, it does have a quantitative definition [12].

Although the true value and error cannot be known exactly, it is in some cases possible to establish a "conventional true value." It occurs if the measurand is a reference standard with a negligible uncertainty in comparison to the uncertainty of the measurement. In such cases, the calibrated value of the reference standard may be considered to be its true value. The difference between the measurement result and this reference

TABLE 1. Unified vocabulary [3].

<table>
<tr><th>Preferred terms</th><th colspan="2">Usage and related non-preferred terms</th></tr>
<tr><td>Process</td><td colspan="2">General term for measurements, measurement processes, machines, and production processes</td></tr>
<tr><td>Uncertainty</td><td>Concept of doubt about a process output</td><td rowspan="5">Related: Accuracy</td></tr>
<tr><td>Standard uncertainty</td><td>Quantity representing uncertainty as a standard deviation</td></tr>
<tr><td>Combined standard uncertainty</td><td>Standard uncertainty in process output, determined by combining standard uncertainty in each influence quantity</td></tr>
<tr><td>Expanded uncertainty</td><td>Standard uncertainty multiplied by a coverage factor for a confidence level</td></tr>
<tr><td>Confidence level</td><td>The level of confidence at which an uncertainty is given</td></tr>
<tr><td>Confidence limits</td><td colspan="2">The limiting values at a given confidence level</td></tr>
<tr><td>Coverage factor (k)</td><td colspan="2">Factor to expand uncertainty to give coverage at a given confidence level for a two-tailed test</td></tr>
<tr><td>z-score</td><td colspan="2">Factor to expand uncertainty to give coverage at a given confidence level for a one-tailed test</td></tr>
<tr><td>Influence quantity</td><td colspan="2">Related: Input quantity, error source, factor</td></tr>
<tr><td>Influence model</td><td colspan="2">New term suggested for mathematical model giving process result in terms of influence quantities. It is used to determine uncertainty.</td></tr>
<tr><td>Error</td><td colspan="2">Unknowable difference between result and true value</td></tr>
<tr><td>Random effects</td><td colspan="2">Related: Random error, common causes, chance causes</td></tr>
<tr><td>Random uncertainty</td><td colspan="2">Related: Precision, common cause variation, chance cause variation</td></tr>
<tr><td>Repeatability</td><td colspan="2">Related: Short-term variability</td></tr>
<tr><td>Reproducibility</td><td colspan="2">Related: Long-term variability</td></tr>
<tr><td>Type A uncertainty</td><td colspan="2">An uncertainty evaluated by statistical analysis of repeated measurements</td></tr>
<tr><td>Systematic effects</td><td colspan="2">Related: Special causes, special cause variation, assignable causes, systematic uncertainty</td></tr>
<tr><td>Bias</td><td colspan="2">Related: Trueness</td></tr>
<tr><td>In statistical control</td><td colspan="2">Corrected result or process with negligible uncorrected systematic effects. Related: Corrected result, stable process</td></tr>
<tr><td>Type B uncertainty</td><td colspan="2">An uncertainty determined by any other means</td></tr>
<tr><td>Specification limits</td><td colspan="2">Related: Tolerance</td></tr>
<tr><td>True pass rate (P_1)</td><td colspan="2">The probability that a product will be in-specification and pass quality control</td></tr>
<tr><td>False pass rate (P_2)</td><td colspan="2">The probability that a product will be out of specification but incorrectly pass quality control</td></tr>
<tr><td>Cost of false pass (C_2)</td><td colspan="2">Cost of a nonconforming unit reaching customer</td></tr>
<tr><td>Conformance limits</td><td colspan="2">Specification limits reduced by $u \cdot k_1$</td></tr>
</table>

value may then be considered to be the error of measurement. Within MSA, this assumption is normally made.

In a general sense, accuracy and uncertainty refer to doubts about the measurement result. Accuracy is in this sense equivalent to uncertainty. So, if a measurement is more accurate, its uncertainty is lower. The GUM defines *uncertainty of measurement* as the specific quantity which measures this. A *standard uncertainty* is this uncertainty given as a standard deviation. Uncertainty can be thought of as giving limiting values within which one can have confidence where the true value lies. Typically, a single standard deviation does not give sufficient confidence. Assuming the uncertainty is characterized by a known probability distribution, limits at a higher confidence level can be calculated by multiplying the standard uncertainty by a *coverage factor* – equivalent to a z-score for a two-sided distribution. Within MSA *accuracy* is the specific quantity representing doubt about the measurement result. It can be confusing as in earlier standards that accuracy meant only trueness. Accuracy is not normally used to calculate confidence limits.

The conventional view is that uncertainty arises from *error sources*. Within the GUM, great care is taken not to confuse error with uncertainty. The term *influence quantities* is, therefore, used for any "quantity that is not the measurand but that affects the result of the measurement." Within SPC, these are called *factors*.

Systematic Effects

Systematic errors are not random and may have a known cause. GUM refers to the *systematic effects* which cause these errors. They arise from the recognized effects of *influence quantities*. If the influence quantity can be quantified, then a correction can be applied to compensate for the effect. In SPC, these effects are now called *special cause variation*. The original work of Walter A. Shewhart – an American physicist, engineer, and statistician considered by some to be the father of statistical – refers to them as *assignable causes* [13]. As discussed, the GUM does not categorize

FIGURE 1. **Cumulative distribution and quantile functions.**

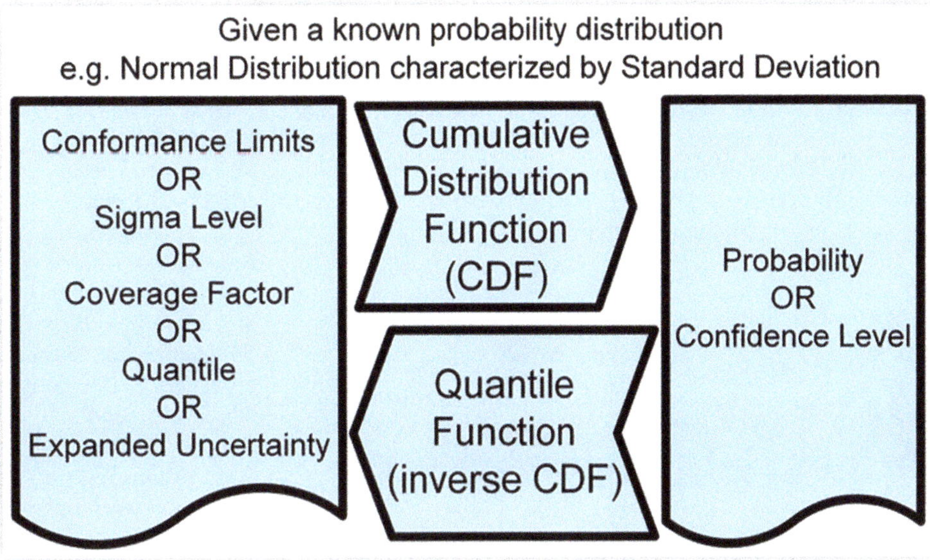

uncertainties by those arising from random or systematic effects. *Type B uncertainties* are those evaluated by means other than the statistical analysis of a series of observations. These uncertainties often, although not necessarily, arise from systematic effects.

The GUM assumes that every effort is made to identify all significant systematic effects and then make corrections for them. SPC makes a similar assumption. SPC calls this a state of *statistical control* or a *stable process*. Only when a process is in control can statistical confidence limits be validly applied. Therefore, obtaining this state of control is central to SPC.

MSA takes a simple approach to systematic effects, by quantifying them and comparing the mean of many measurements with a reference value. The difference is the *bias*, also called *trueness*. MSA defines accuracy as the combination of precision and trueness. It assumes that the systematic effect of uncertainty in the reference standard is negligible. It is, therefore, suited to measurements further down the traceability chain but cannot be applied to fundamental standards. However, MSA does have a role in interlaboratory comparisons of standards [14]. Within the GUM, it is preferred that any identifiable bias has been corrected. However, in cases where this is not practical, the uncertainty and bias may be combined (GUM F.2.4.5) to give something equivalent to the accuracy quantity used in MSA. Key differences are that the uncertainty incorporates the uncertainty in the reference standard and that the quantities are not usually combined into a single parameter. Although the MSA approach does not depend on all systematic effects being compensated, it is still recommended that any systematic effects are small compared to random effects [9].

The proper consideration of systematic effects often requires Type B evaluation of uncertainty, something discussed in full in the following domain.

Why This Domain Remains Unresolved

Very little effort has been made to harmonize the equivalent methodologies. They are often seen as performing discrete functions for which a specialized approach appears appropriate. The fact that both MSA and SPC use incomplete representations of uncertainties is not well understood by those practicing these disciplines within the industry. Furthermore, metrologists may assume that uncertainty evaluation could be applied within manufacturing if there was a desire to do this within the industry. However, issues around determining intrinsic and expected uncertainties would first need to be resolved.

Recommendations

A unified uncertainty framework will require a standardized vocabulary, suggested here as a subset of the VIM [11], with the addition of concepts of statistical control and conformance limits. In tabulating the initial vocabulary, the equivalence of terms in common usage within other methodologies has also been noted. Table 1 gives an example of some important terms in this vocabulary.

It is also useful to clarify the relationship between

1. Conformance limits, sigma levels, coverage factors, quantiles, and expanded uncertainty

and their inverse:

2. Probability and confidence level.

Assuming a known probability distribution, the *cumulative distribution function* (CDF) is required to obtain one of the second quantities given as one of the first. The reverse operation is the inverse CDF or quantile function. This relationship is illustrated in Figure 1.

A working group should be formed involving technical experts from within both the industry and fundamental metrology research. This group should establish a unified vocabulary, perhaps similar to that given above, as well as attempt to integrate emerging solutions within the other unresolved domains, discussed below, into a comprehensive uncertainty framework. Doing so will enable system-wide optimization of production systems.

Evaluating Type B Uncertainties in Industrial Measurements

A model-based approach, such as the uncertainty framework given in the GUM [4], enables both observable and unobservable uncertainties to be included to give a *combined uncertainty*. Uncertainties which can be directly observed by the statistical analysis of repeated measurements are known as *Type A*. Uncertainties which are not practical to observe in this way are obtained by some other means, and referred to as *Type B*. Common examples of Type B uncertainties include the uncertainties of reference values, obtained from calibration certificates, and the uncertainties of material properties, obtained from material specifications. To combine these uncertainties, a mathematical model is required. This may be a function giving the measurement result in terms of the influence quantities, or some algorithm which produces the same effect. Influence quantities may be nominally zero with some random uncertainty, such as repeatability or rounding errors. They may also be correction values such as an environmental measurement or calibration offset, which have a nominal value as well as an uncertainty about this value.

One reason why Type B uncertainties are required is that a large number of influence quantities, or factors, may affect the variability of a measurement result. It can make it impractical to design an experiment which is sensitive to all of them. Even if it were possible to perform the required number of replicate measurements, certain factors may be very difficult to vary in a random way during a gauge study. For example, there is uncertainty in the calibration of a reference standard, but it would be very difficult to obtain many different reference standards which have randomly varying calibration errors [15].

The GUM, originally published in 1995, is intended to provide a universal framework for many areas including "maintaining quality control and quality assurance in production" [16]. However, within the industry, the evaluation of measurements is still usually carried out using MSA, as recommended in Six Sigma[8] and involving *gauge studies* [9]. It does not require a mathematical model of the measurement, instead of relying on designed experiments to observe the effect of random and systematic effects on the measurement result. Type B uncertainties cannot, therefore, be included; and, if these are significant, MSA will indicate that the *accuracy* of a measurement is significantly better than its actual uncertainty. Some precautions are normally taken, such as attempting to ensure that the calibration uncertainty is negligible. Doing so may not, however, always be possible and other Type B uncertainties may easily be overlooked. MSA is, therefore, less rigorous than the GUM approach.

A common misconception within the industry is that MSA gives a more robust evaluation of the accuracy of measurements than uncertainty evaluation. Between 2010 and 2014, the author was part of a project which worked with 235 small manufacturing companies and four world-leading aerospace prime contractors/manufacturers. This project, which was funded by the European Regional Development Fund, was called The Laboratory for Integrated Metrology Applications Business Technology Centre. At least two days were spent working to understand each company's measurement methods and requirements. This research revealed a widespread mistrust of uncertainty evaluation, which is seen as being theoretical, within the industry. The preferred evaluation is usually a gauge Repeatability and Reproducibility (gauge R&R) study. The gauge R&R study is believed to give the "true accuracy" of a measurement process given that it is based on experimental observations. The importance of Type B uncertainties is not widely understood.

Consider an example of how systematic effects may go unnoticed in a gauge R&R study. A study may consider that thermal expansion is a significant influence on measurements. The measurement process, therefore, includes a correction for thermal expansion, and a gauge R&R study is carried out carefully ensuring that the temperature is varied in a way that represents historical data for the measurement area. It may appear that thermal expansion has been properly accounted for; however, consider that all the parts used in the study come from the same batch of material, which happens to have a coefficient of thermal expansion (CTE) close to the nominal value for this material. The problem here is that material CTE has significant uncertainty (discussed further below); therefore, when parts are made from a different batch of material, the measurements will vary significantly when the temperature varies, even though a correction is being made. This is an example of an influence quantity – in this case, the uncertainty in the CTE – which is extremely difficult to vary realistically in a gauge R&R study. Therefore, some influence quantities may need to be quantified using a Type B evaluation and then combined using an uncertainty evaluation approach.

Although a number of different methodologies remain common within the industry, significant steps have been taken toward applying the GUM uncertainty framework within industrial measurement. ISO 14253-2 "Geometrical product specifications (GPS) – Inspection by measurement of workpieces and measuring equipment" from the International Organization for Standardization (ISO) [17] provides a simplified guide to uncertainty evaluation, which is intended to be more accessible to an industrial audience than the highly mathematical terms in which the

GUM presents these methods. ISO 14253-2 also addresses the difficulties that may arise when attempting to obtain individual uncertainty estimates for many influence quantities with something it calls the Procedure for Uncertainty MAnagement (PUMA).

PUMA is an iterative approach which enables quick worst-case estimates to be used for many influences, with more rigorous estimates only required for critical values. PUMA is discussed in more detail with respect to obtaining standard industrial uncertainty models below.

VDA-5, Capability of Measurement Processes, Capability of Measuring Systems [18], published by the German Association of the Automotive Industry (Verband Der Automobilindustrie, or VDA), combines uncertainty evaluation with MSA's gauge studies. An uncertainty budget is used which considers all influences on the measurement and a gauge R&R study is used to quantify the random uncertainty within this budget. It also explains how attribute gauges, which give a binary pass/fail result, can be evaluated using an uncertainty budget. Influences which VDA-5 states should be considered include uncertainty of the reference standard, resolution, repeatability, environmental effects, operator, test part, and many others. The uncertainty aspects are based on the GUM, while the MSA procedures are taken from the Automotive Industry Action Group (AIAG) *MSA Manual* [9].

By focusing on uncertainty budgets, ISO 14253-2 and VDA-5 are not the state of the art in uncertainty evaluation. Uncertainty budgets are a way of implementing the *law of uncertainty propagation*, as given in the GUM. The first supplement to the GUM [19] has pointed out that this "law" is an approximation which should be validated using numerical simulations. However, for most practical purposes, uncertainty budgets provide an acceptable approximation, and in practice they are rarely validated by simulation.

It may appear that standards such as ISO 14253-2 and VDA-5 provide an acceptable method for evaluating Type B uncertainties in industrial measurements, and in many cases they will. However, under some circumstances, important Type B uncertainties cannot be modeled by the GUM approach. The GUM is only intended to provide the uncertainty of an individual measurement, for which all input quantities are known. The industry typically wants to know a generalized uncertainty for any measurement carried out in a measurement process.

VDA-5 assumes that the GUM approach will work in this way without modification. However, if the measurement includes correction values, then this assumption may not be correct. For example, if a dimensional measurement is corrected for thermal expansion, the uncertainty budget should include a Type B uncertainty for the part's CTE. The contribution that this uncertainty makes to the combined uncertainty of measurement is determined by its sensitivity coefficient, which is a function of the correction value itself. It will be different for each measurement, meaning the uncertainty will be different. If we want an expected uncertainty, which could be used to infer probability of false decisions within the process, then we need to model the interaction between variation in the correction value and uncertainty in the CTE. These interactions are not included in any standard methods for uncertainty evaluation. The unresolved domain of determining *expected uncertainty* is explored in more detail in a following section.

Recommendations

The primary barrier to rigorous evaluation of industrial measurement uncertainty is a lack of awareness. The fact that, by omitting Type B sources, MSA can significantly underestimate uncertainty needs to be communicated more clearly within the quality engineering community.

The issue of how to evaluate expected uncertainty for measurement processes must also be addressed for a model-based approach to be fully adopted. It will then be possible to make valid capability statements which consider effects that cannot be directly observed in gauge study results.

Evaluating Intrinsic Uncertainty

Product specifications are typically continuous, while measurements can only be made at a finite number of discrete points. It means that even if the measurements had no uncertainty, there would be uncertainty about the regions between the measurements. The GUM refers to it as *intrinsic uncertainty*, but current methods do not account for it when making decisions about product conformance. The GUM makes the assumption that intrinsic uncertainty results from imprecision in specifications. However, correct Geometric Dimensioning and Tolerancing [20, 21] precisely specifies the form of products, providing zones within which all points on a surface must lie. The issue is that it is impossible to verify fully such conditions using a finite number of measurements.

One suggested approach is to use Gaussian processes [22] to estimate the uncertainty for regions between measured points. This approach makes an assumption that the feature being measured departs from its nominal geometry in a random way that can be characterized by a probability function. The variation in the measured points is considered, together with the uncertainty of these measurements, to give a function for the continuous uncertainty of the feature. This approach is relatively new and there is very little awareness of it within the industry. Most significantly, it has not been validated against real industrial measurements to test the validity of assumptions made.

It is also important to note that observing patterns in high-resolution data can provide a lot of diagnostic information. Additional benefits can be derived from high-resolution data, beyond simply reducing intrinsic uncertainty.

Random Effects

Random errors are those that change every time a measurement is repeated due to unpredictable effects, which may vary with factors such as time or position. The GUM refers to the *random effects* which cause these errors. It notes that they cannot be compensated, but they may be reduced by averaging a number of measurements. MSA refers to *random error*, while SPC uses *common causes* or, from Shewhart's original work, *chance causes* [13]. These concepts are equivalent.

As discussed, individual errors are unknown, though random effects can be quantified by statistical analysis of repeated measurements. It is usually done by calculating the standard deviation. MSA refers to this as *precision*. The GUM refers to the uncertainty characterizing a *random effect*. Both GUM and MSA make the distinction between *repeatability* and *reproducibility*. Within SPC, they are called *short-term variability* and *long-term variability*, respectively. Repeatability is the uncertainty resulting from random effects under the same conditions. Reproducibility is the uncertainty resulting from random effects under changed conditions. The conditions which may change include those of the operator, instrument, time of measurement, calibration, environment, or any other significant condition. Within MSA, the focus tends to be on the part being measured and the operator carrying out the measurement. For SPC, the focus tends to be on time. In uncertainty evaluation, the recommendation is to model the effects of all possible influences to determine those that may be significant.

The GUM acknowledges the existence of random and systematic effects. However, it recommends that uncertainties are not categorized in this way. This is because a random effect present when calibrating a reference will become a systematic effect when that standard is used to calibrate another instrument. To avoid this confusion, the GUM identifies Type A uncertainties which are evaluated by statistical analysis of repeated observations.

Recommendations

Step-by-step procedures supported by readily usable equations, or algorithms, are first needed to enable industrial trials of Gaussian processes for the evaluation of intrinsic uncertainty. Trials should then be carried out which validate the assumptions of this approach by comparing predicted surface uncertainties based on a small number of measurement points with high-resolution scanning measurements. This approach should enable the validity of Gaussian processes to be established for specific types of industrial processes. Only at that stage will it be possible to decide whether an alternative approach is required, or whether the suggested approach should be standardized for industrial use.

Ultimately, algorithms able to model intrinsic uncertainty may be used to control intelligent inspection processes. Such an approach could perform an initial rapid inspection and determine whether it gives sufficient confidence to accept or reject. If the intrinsic uncertainty means that neither conformance nor nonconformance can be established, then additional measurement would be automatically carried out. Where quality issues are detected, inspection processes must also ensure that sufficient data has been obtained to support subsequent root cause analysis.

Evaluating Expected Uncertainty: Uncertainties in Correction Values when Predicting Uncertainty in Processes

The GUM approach requires a mathematical model giving the measurement result in terms of its input quantities. To determine the uncertainty of the result, the uncertainties of the input quantities must be known, and for nonlinear measurement models, the values of these input quantities must also be known. It means that the GUM method can generally only be properly applied to the *after-the-fact* evaluation of uncertainty [23].

The evaluation of measurements used for quality control in production is frequently carried out in a general sense, for an instrument or measurement process, rather than a specific measurement. The two primary reasons for this practice are to determine whether the measurement system is capable and to set fixed conformance limits. The setting of fixed conformance limits is an avoidable convenience, since uncertainty should properly be evaluated and conformance limits can be set for each individual measurement result. The evaluation of instrument capability is necessary for the economic planning of both production systems and scientific experiments. Although the use of fixed capability indices may be replaced by more optimal cost minimization approaches [24, 25], it remains necessary to evaluate the anticipated uncertainty of an instrument or process. In such cases, specific values for input quantities are not yet known, although they may be expressed as a probability distribution. The GUM method, therefore, cannot be properly applied to nonlinear models because there is no way of expressing sensitivities in terms of these probability distributions (which will be demonstrated using an example later in this section).

Estimating the *expected uncertainty* of a measurement, when its input quantities are not yet known, is defined here as *before-the-fact* evaluation. In practice, uncertainties are often estimated before the fact with one of two approaches typically used:

1. Where likely deviations from the nominal value of an input quantity have a negligible effect on uncertainty, the nominal value is used. This approximation is perfectly acceptable because it has a negligible effect on the resulting uncertainty.

2. Where likely deviations of an input quantity have a significant effect on uncertainty, its worst case value is used [17]. This approach is not a rigorous method for the *before-the-fact* evaluation of uncertainty, and it can result in significant errors in uncertainty estimation.

More commonly for industrial measurements, only a gauge R&R study is used and there is no attempt to evaluate Type B uncertainty. It is unlikely that all the significant sources of uncertainty can be properly evaluated within a properly designed experiment. Such an experiment would need to have sensitivity to any variation in the measurement result caused by interactions between influence quantities. If such an experiment is able to capture the effect of variation in any input quantities, as well as errors in their measurement, then it will give a valid representation of the expected uncertainty. However, where a measurement model is sufficiently complex that variation in an input quantity has a significant effect on uncertainty, it is very unlikely that it can be properly evaluated without Type B uncertainties and a model-based approach. Furthermore, the VDA-5 approach does not enable variation in input quantities to be included within the uncertainty propagation model.

Supplement one to the GUM (GUM-S1) uses a MCS which avoids many of the analytical approximations of the GUM. It does, however, still require known input quantities. Before-the-fact evaluation, therefore, requires the same approximations as the GUM method described above. It is, however, possible to extend the GUM-S1 methods to properly evaluate *expected uncertainty* using Markov chain MCS. A summary of the GUM and GUM-S1 methods are first presented below, followed by extension of the GUM-S1 method to enable before-the-fact evaluation of expected uncertainty.

To understand the difficulty with applying the GUM to *before-the-fact* evaluation, consider a simple example involving a correction for thermal expansion ΔL calculated using the equation:

$$\Delta L = \alpha \Delta T L \quad (1)$$

where α is the CTE, ΔT is the difference between the measured temperature of the part and the reference temperature, and L is the measured length of the part.

The GUM specifies that the combined uncertainty is obtained using the law of propagation of uncertainty. For this example, to a first-order approximation, the uncertainty of the correction would, therefore, be given by

$$u^2(\Delta L) \approx (\alpha \Delta T u(L))^2 + (L \Delta T u(\alpha))^2 + (L\alpha u(\Delta T))^2 \quad (2)$$

where $u(x)$ is the uncertainty of x.

Each term in this equation contains the uncertainty of one of the input quantities, together with the actual values for the remaining input quantities. A current practice is to either use a worst case or a nominal value for each input quantity, as discussed above. The CTE, α, will most likely be a Type B uncertainty obtained from a material specification; therefore, its value will be known in advance. Because it will not vary from measurement to measurement, its nominal value is used. For a given part dimension, the length L will typically only vary by a small fraction of its nominal value; therefore, changes in L will have a negligible effect on the combined uncertainty and, again, the nominal value may be used.

Issues with the current practice only arise when we consider the temperature offset ΔT. This may have a nominal value of zero and vary either side of this by a significant amount, according to the environment where the measurement takes place. The nominal value, therefore, only relates to the case where no temperature offset is detected. In this case, uncertainty in the CTE would not result in any uncertainty in the correction, since no correction would be applied. Using the nominal value is, therefore, clearly not appropriate here. If, on the other hand, a worst-case value is used for ΔT, then the uncertainty estimate would also be a worst-case value, not the statistically determined *expected uncertainty*. It might at first appear that a reasonable estimate could be obtained by using the standard deviation in the actual temperature offset (not the standard uncertainty of its measurement) in place of the nominal value. It is shown later that this does not always provide such as good estimate as it might at first appear.

In the case of the GUM-S1 method, Equation (1) would be evaluated m times. For each evaluation, the nominal or measured values would be perturbed by randomly generated values drawn from the probability distributions for the uncertainty of each term. The GUM-S1 does not provide for a method of also perturbing these parameters to account for variation in their true values. This method cannot, therefore, be directly applied to evaluate expected uncertainty. Although a true value cannot be measured, it does exist and can be considered within a simulation.

In order to simulate the effect of variation in the values of influence quantities, the expected variation must be quantified. These can be represented as probability distributions, describing our uncertainty about what value these quantities might take at the time of measurement. It is then possible to simulate both the true value of the measurement, considering the propagation of the influence quantities' true values, and the measurement result, simulating both true values and measurement errors. In this way, the measurement error can be simulated for each iteration in the MCS. The simulation result, therefore, gives m measurement errors which represent the expected uncertainty.

Such an approach has yet to be standardized or widely accepted as a means of using a model-based uncertainty evaluation to determine measurement capability.

Modeling Expected Variation of Manufacturing Processes

Two fundamental approaches to evaluating the validity of measurement results are currently used: the model-based

FIGURE 2. **Comparison of measurement and production process.**

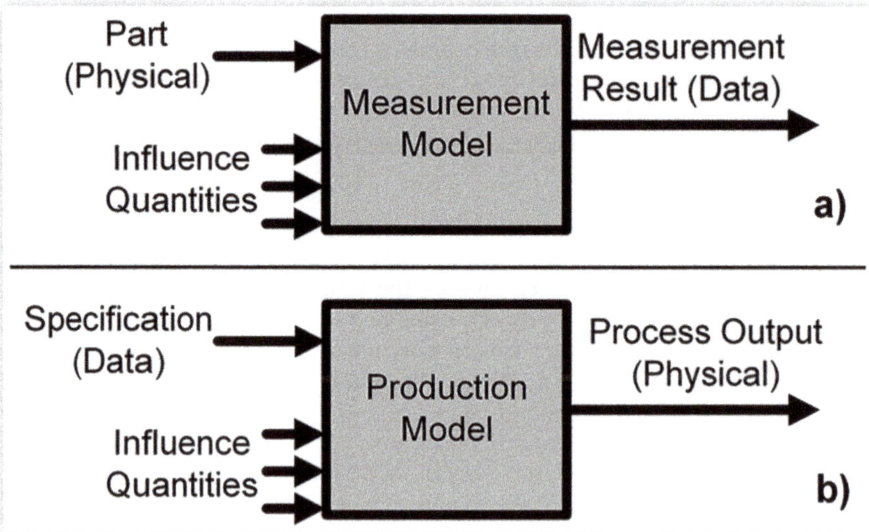

approach of evaluating uncertainty of measurement and the data-based approach of MSA. The advantage of uncertainty evaluation is that it allows any available data to be evaluated using all the statistical analysis methods available in MSA, but also any unobserved systematic effects to be considered as Type B uncertainties.

For manufacturing processes, the model-based or uncertainty evaluation approach is less well established. In fact, the model-based approach cannot currently be directly applied to processes because uncertainty evaluation has only been explicitly defined for after-the-fact evaluation of measurements.

Once extended to model variation in influence quantities, model-based uncertainty evaluation may then be applied to production processes as well as measurement. It is likely to enable significantly increased confidence in processes, reducing not only rework and scrap but also the need for product verification measurements. Instead, it will be possible to monitor influence quantities, applying real-time correction and only measuring the product when the process confidence is low.

Although before-the-fact evaluation of uncertainty makes a model-based approach suitable for production processes, a fundamental difference between a measurement and a production process remains with respect to Type A evaluations. For a measurement, the same object may be measured multiple times, then the standard deviation calculated directly from the results. Therefore, when evaluating uncertainty of measurement, the input is a physical object and the output is data. For a production process, the input is data, the specification, and the output is a physical object. Therefore, to determine the Type A uncertainty for a production process, each output must be measured using a separate measurement process, which also has uncertainty (Figure 2).

The observed variation for a production process is, therefore, a combination of the process variation and the measurement uncertainty. Given a sufficient number of observations, any random effects can be separated using analysis of variance (ANOVA). Any remaining systematic uncertainty cannot be separated, and some uncertainty is brought into the process from the measurement – equivalent to including the uncertainty of a reference standard in a calibration uncertainty.

Recommendations

A method for the before-the-fact MCS of expected uncertainty has been suggested. Such an approach should be first academically formalized so that uncertainty evaluation can be applied comprehensively to the consideration of uncertainty of measurement and processes within manufacturing. These methods should then undergo industrial trials in order to create robust and practical standards.

Standard Industrial Uncertainty Models

A significant practical barrier to applying model-based uncertainty evaluation within the industry is the need for mathematical models describing how the measurement result is effected by influence quantities. The gauge studies used within MSA have the advantage of being easily packaged into standard procedures which can be followed and the data entered into software to give a result.

For one-dimensional instruments subjected to environmental influences, uncertainty can be evaluated by relatively simple standard uncertainty budgets, as suggested in VDA-5 [18], together with the PUMA, as defined in ISO 14253-2 [17]. PUMA involves initially using only easily obtainable values for the uncertainty of influence quantities, including worst-case estimates where more accurate estimates would be difficult to obtain. Where this results in a combined uncertainty that is fit for purpose, or where individual sources do not contribute significantly to the combined uncertainty, no further evaluation is required. It can then be an iterative process in which more accurate estimates and/or reductions in uncertainty are obtained only for the dominant sources of uncertainty, until an acceptable estimate is obtained.

For more complex measurements and processes, these solutions do not go far enough. A modular tool kit of mathematical models and algorithms is, therefore, required to enable such systems to be readily modeled without creating a mathematical model of the measurement instrument or process from first-principles every time. Many models have already been described within the academic literature for complex instruments [26, 27] and machines [28]. In many cases algorithms are also in the public domain, yet they are not available in standard formats and not compiled into comprehensive libraries, making industrial application very difficult. Measurement software, such as SpatialAnalyzer from New River Kinematics, do contain some standard uncertainty models for instruments, but these are highly simplified and do not address any of the technical challenges identified in this report.

Another important consideration is the double counting of uncertainties. For example, Type B evaluation may be used for an effect that has already been observed within a repeatability study. Interactions between geometric effects may also lead to double counting. Checks must be carried out to minimize this type of overestimation.

Recommendations

Significant work is required to compile, develop, and create modular uncertainty models, including

1. Instrument and machine elements
2. Environmental effects
3. Datum structures
4. Intrinsic uncertainty

Algorithms will also be required which enable nonstandard distributions and variation in correction values to be propagated through these models. Significant work will be required to create standards that enable complete models to be constructed from the modular components and then run through these algorithms, supporting PUMA. The possibility of using deep learning to construct empirical models from large datasets also warrants further investigation, although the significance of Type B evaluation should not be lost in this process.

Validating Industrial Uncertainty Models

A mistrust of model-based uncertainty exists within the industry. It is the only means of including all sources of uncertainty, yet it is also open to human error because it is only as good as the mathematical model of the measurement. A complex mathematical model, if incorrect, can significantly increase or decrease the effect of influences. There is also a risk that important influences may be overlooked and not included in the measurement model.

For these reasons, a model-based evaluation of uncertainty should be validated experimentally as far as is practically possible. In Section 3.4.3 of the GUM, such an approach is described thus:

In order to decide if a measurement system is functioning properly, the experimentally observed variability of its output values, as measured by their observed standard deviation, is often compared with the predicted standard deviation obtained by combining the various uncertainty components that characterize the measurement. In such cases, only those components (whether obtained from Type A or Type B evaluations) that could contribute to the experimentally observed variability of these output values should be considered [4].

It is logical that, in deciding which sources have contributed to the observed variation, some influences may contribute, but not so to the full extent of their uncertainty. Therefore, what is really being suggested here is that

1. A reproducibility study is carried out which considers all significant influences and attempts to ensure that they are varied in a way that as far as possible represents their uncertainty.
2. The anticipated variation in measurement results is calculated, using the same mathematical model used for calculating the uncertainty of measurement. Rather than using the uncertainty of each influence quantity, the extent of variation present during the repeatability study is used.

Such an approach appears sensible. However, the brief section of the GUM that describes it does not consider the challenges of designing experiments are able to properly represent the interactions between large numbers of influences. In fact, it is one of the reasons why a model-based uncertainty evaluation may be required. Significant related work has been carried out to validate uncertainty statements using interlaboratory comparisons [29, 30, 31, 32], yet very little consideration has been given to how industrial uncertainty models should be validated.

Recommendations

Before an uncertainty framework can be adopted for industrial measurement, robust methods of validating uncertainty models will be required. It will first require a theoretical framework based on experimental design and the methods used in interlaboratory comparisons. Standardized industrial procedures will then be needed, supported by algorithms which enable experimental data to be compared with standard uncertainty models. Tests performed under reduced reproducibility conditions will then provide confidence that the production system will behave as predicted by uncertainty models under the actual conditions of operation. Such an approach should acknowledge that Type B uncertainties cannot be fully validated while also stressing that, when properly validated, uncertainty evaluation is more reliable than a gauge study.

Summarizing and Extrapolating from MCS

One of the issues with the GUM is that it makes assumptions about linearity and normality which can sometimes lead to inaccurate uncertainty statements. What makes this particularly problematic is that it is very difficult to quantify these effects, which can result in significant underestimation of uncertainty at high confidence levels [23]. Moving into Industry 4.0, such limitations are detrimental and a higher fidelity "virtual systems approach" must be disseminated as algorithms rather than equations [33]. Supplement One to the GUM (GUM-S1), published in 2007 [19], addresses these issues. By using MCS, it avoids making any assumptions about linearity or the probability distribution for the combined uncertainty of the measurement. An attempt can be made to fit standard distributions to the simulation results, and if this output is found to be Gaussian, or some other standard distribution, then the results can be summarized using parameters such as the standard deviation.

If the output distribution does not follow a standard probability distribution, then expanded uncertainties, equivalent to confidence intervals, can be directly extracted from the simulation results. It is simply a matter of sorting the simulation results and counting the *n*th value to determine a quantile. This approach depends on a sufficient number of simulation trials. Where simulations produce a nonstandard probability distribution, there are two unresolved issues:

1. How can a nonstandard distribution be summarized and recreated so that expanded uncertainties at arbitrary confidence levels may later be obtained, perhaps for optimization, and so the distribution can be used as an input to some system-level simulation at a later date.
2. How can high-confidence extrapolations be made from a nonstandard distribution. For example, to determine the Six-Sigma limits of a process, with a reasonable degree of accuracy, would require approximately 100 observations to be outside of these limits. It would require approximately 10^9 MCS, which can become computationally unfeasible for complex measurement models or use within an optimization algorithm.

GUMS1's references to the propagation of distributions are limited to the first two moments (the mean and standard deviation) and do not consider parametric distributions characterized by higher order statistics, such as skewness, kurtosis, etc. The issue of summarizing distributions has been approached in a number of ways. The conventional approach is to select from a wider library of standard distributions and fit using higher-order statistics. For example, including skewness and kurtosis in addition to the mean and standard deviation. Attempts have been made to find the best fit by selecting higher-order parametric distributions such as from the entire family of Pearson distributions, as well as Tukey's Lambda and *gh* distributions [34]. Some alternative approaches include fitting splines to quantiles [35], using higher-order Taylor Series expansions to model skewness and kurtosis [36] and determining confidence levels using the Cornish-Fisher expansion [37].

There has not been an extensive comparison to determine the relative appropriateness of these methods under different circumstances. Comparisons between methods have focused on differences between moments and cumulants at low confidence levels [38, 39]. This ignores a key benefit of distribution fitting methods over MCS: the ability to determine the probability of rare events. What constitutes a rare event depends on the complexity of the measurement model, availability of computational power, and time available to obtain the result. For simple functional models, the probability of a $1{:}10^5$ event can be simulated in less than one second. However, for a measurement involving a least-squares solution for a coordinate transformation, it would take several minutes to determine the probability of a $1{:}10^3$ event.

Recommendations

Methods of summarizing probability distributions should be evaluated, giving consideration to the requirements of industrial metrology. Highly skewed and high-kurtosis distributions should be used, which have been generated by simulation of real industrial measurement and production systems. Using these distributions, methods should be compared in terms of their ability to produce random draws for input into further simulation and efficiently determine CDFs and quantiles at high confidence levels. There should also be some consideration of their ability to provide intuitive communication of the distribution.

Make Optimal Product Verification Decisions

Capability indices do not make optimal selections of instruments and machines. A capability index in theory states whether an instrument is capable of proving conformance or controlling a process. In practice, industrial engineers are frequently required to select from several instruments, all of which either may be capable or may not be capable. In such cases, decisions must be based on a consideration of what is "good enough" and what level of expenditure is justified. Although rigorous statistical analysis may be involved in determining capability, the resulting decisions are, therefore, currently made in subjective and inconsistent ways.

The purpose of quantifying measurement uncertainty and process variation is to inform decisions regarding the optimization of the production system. There will always be a degree of trade-off between cost and quality. Methods currently used in the industry typically provide target values for quality metrics with little regard to the specific trade-off for the process under consideration. For example, VDA-5 states that an instrument's expanded uncertainty, at 95% confidence, should be less than 15% of the product's tolerance [18]. Similarly, ISO 14253-1 states that specified tolerances should be reduced by the expanded uncertainty to determine conformance limits [40], typically at 95% confidence. In both cases, no consideration is given to the significant probability of false decisions or the costs that result from false decisions.

It has been suggested [24, 25, 41, 42] that an optimal approach to this trade-off is to minimize the costs associated with production, measurement, and nonconformance. Because it has already been shown that current methods of modeling uncertainty in measurement and production processes are incomplete and inconsistent, methods of optimizing the system using uncertainty are also incomplete.

As an example of an optimal decision algorithm, consider the initial configuration of a production system to manufacture a part. It involves selecting the production process, the measurement process, and the confidence level at which parts are accepted. A number of potential processes are assumed to be known to the manufacturer with uncertainty models and costs available.

For each combination of production and measurement process, and inspection confidence level, two conditional probabilities are determined:

- P_1, the probability that a product will be in-specification and pass quality control, a "true negative"
- P_2, the probability that a product will be out of specification, but pass quality control due to a measurement error (a "false negative").

Each part has a fixed cost of manufacture, C_1, and only parts that pass quality control generate income. Defective parts reaching the customer incur an additional quality cost C_2 in the form of concessions, loss of reputation, and potential liability [24]. Considering these costs and probabilities together, the quality-adjusted cost per part sold may be calculated:

$$C_Q = \frac{C_1 + P_2 C_2}{P_1 + P_2} \tag{3}$$

An optimal production system minimizes this cost. It is achieved by selecting a production process, an inspection process, and a confidence level for conformance limits. These parameters are optimized in a two-stage process. Every combination of production process and inspection process is considered in turn. An additional possibility is to not measure the final project, relying on confidence in the manufacturing process; this option is also included in the combinations from which a selection is made. For each combination, the conformance limits are optimized to minimize the cost. The combination that gives the lowest cost is then selected.

For the above example, if uncertainties follow standard distributions, the conditional probabilities can be determined using a bivariate CDF. Where MCS produces nonstandard distributions, the probabilities can be determined by direct extension of the simulation. However, where the cost of a concession is very high, meaning that very small probabilities produce significant expected costs, then direct simulation becomes computationally infeasible, highlighting the need for methods of extrapolating from numerical simulations, as indicated above. It has been explained that an *expected uncertainty*, obtained *before the fact*, must be treated somewhat differently to the uncertainty of a measurement as defined by GUM. This often results in non-Gaussian output distributions. Further work is, therefore, required to standardize these methods and create industrial procedures.

Recommendations

A rational goal for quality engineering is to minimize the quality-adjusted cost per unit of product sold to the customer. Such an approach requires compatible methods of evaluating uncertainty in both production and inspection processes. Quality optimization algorithms should be developed, which select production processes and measurement instruments, and set conformance limits to maximize profitability. These novel algorithms will use conditional probabilities, determined from parametric distributions fitted to higher-order moments or cumulants. They will consider costs of production, inspection, and passing defective products to the customer. They will also allow for multiple quality metrics with differing levels of defect resulting in differing quality costs, the cost of reworking, and production delay costs.

A major challenge in adopting such an approach will be obtaining sufficiently accurate and detailed estimates of the costs associated with quality defects. A challenge will be to justify this effort in terms of the benefit that will be gained. It may, however, be argued that, even if based on approximate estimated costs, such an approach provides a more rational basis for decisions than one which does not consider the cost implications of quality at all.

Make Optimal Process Control Decisions

The control of production processes using SPC is somewhat beyond the scope of industrial metrology, going somewhat further into the field of industrial statistics. However, some lessons certainly can be learned from metrology within SPC. Most notably, the combination of uncertainties and the determination of uncertainty components by Type B means can generally be carried out for a measurement or a production process in exactly the same way. When evaluating an uncertainty by repeated measurement (a Type A evaluation) there is, however, a fundamental difference between a measurement and a production process. The same object may be measured multiple times, then the standard deviation calculated directly from the results. For the evaluation of uncertainty for a measurement, the input is a physical object and the output is data. For a production process, it is reversed. The input of a production process is data, the specification. A production process then outputs a physical object. Therefore, to determine the Type A uncertainty for a production process, each output must be measured using a separate measurement process, which also has uncertainty – as was noted in the previous section on evaluating expected uncertainty.

Recommendations

As an industrial uncertainty framework becomes established, opportunities will arise for uncertainty models to be exploited within the process control. Before-the-fact evaluation of expected uncertainty and the evaluation of Type B uncertainties have direct application in production processes, as well as measurements. Potential also exists for uncertainty models to be used for the *recalibration of production systems* using feedback from product measurements to adjust production machines via model parameters.

Conclusions

The creation of an industrial uncertainty framework that enables cost-optimal trade-offs to be made within production systems will be an enormous undertaking requiring global collaborations. A number of primary areas of activity are required to bring about such a paradigm shift for quality engineering: the resolution of technical challenges at the fundamental and theoretical level, the agreement of standardized methods and terminology, the education of practicing engineers, and the development of software tools.

An initial framework must first be agreed upon through collaborative research between academics, industrial end users, and the National Measurement Institutes. It should provide the direction for further work, much of which has already been set out in this report. Initial unification of the terminology and methods of current MSA, SPC, and uncertainty evaluation should also be carried out at this stage.

Fundamental research is then required to agree on methods of uncertainty evaluation that are suited to both after-the-fact evaluation of measurements and before-the-fact evaluation of processes. These methods must allow for Type B and intrinsic uncertainties. Methods of constructing uncertainty models from a standard library of influence quantities will be required for uncertainty evaluation to have widespread application within the industry. The propagation of uncertainty should be carried out using numerical simulation, to avoid the approximations with the GUM's analytical methods. However, it will require methods of summarizing and extrapolating from non-Gaussian output distributions.

Once the fundamental issues related to uncertainty modeling of industrial processes has been resolved, greater engagement from industrial users will be vital. Extensive case studies should be used to develop practical methods of modeling processes while populating the library of influence quantities. It will then be possible to start standardizing the methods and developing educational programs to instill the required understanding.

The final challenge will be in applying the understanding of uncertainty to a cost-based optimization of production systems. The major change will be in moving from a simple pass-or-fail model of product specifications to one which fully considers the cost implications of quality defects.

SAE EDGE™ Research Reports

SAE EDGE™ Research Reports, like the present report on "Unsettled Technology Domains in Industrial Metrology," are intended to push further out into still unsettled areas of technology of interest to the mobility industry. SAE launches these reports before attempting to form a joint working group, let alone a Cooperative Research Program or a Standards Committee.

SAE EDGE™ Research Reports are intended to be quick, concise overviews of major unsettled areas where vital new technologies are emerging. By definition, an unsettled area is characterized more by confusion and controversy than established order. Early practitioners must confront an absence of agreement. Their challenge is often not to seize the high ground but to find common ground. These scouting reports from the frontiers of investigation are intended merely to begin the process of sorting through critical issues, contributing to a better understanding of key problems, and providing helpful suggestions about possible next steps and avenues of investigation.

SAE EDGE™ Research Reports, therefore, are fundamentally distinct from the more formal working groups approach and far removed from the more mature Cooperative Research Program and standard's development process. They begin by convening an informal meeting of subject matter experts working in an unsettled area of technology from the industry, government, and the research community. A moderated but collegial discussion ensues regarding their shared interest. This conversation attempts to identify critical issues hindering a clear understanding of important topics, preventing a common agreement on potential solutions, or slowing progress in key areas of research.

An SAE EDGE™ Research Report is then drafted and circulated for comment to meeting attendees and other interested parties. After review, the final result of this process is a report like the current examination of unsettled issues concerning the sensors needed for automated vehicles.

Next Steps for Industrial Metrology

This publication should be considered only as a first step toward clarifying the issues around industrial metrology. The intention behind this and other SAE EDGE™ Research Reports is to start a dialogue among interested parties on important industry-wide topics that require further attention. The expectation is that these explorations of unsettled areas of technology will lead to the formation of working groups and, ultimately, committees that can address and resolve the issues they raise, producing a framework for developing a common vocabulary of definitions, best practices, protocols, and standards needed to support continued progress toward safer and more innovative automotive products.

The experts' meeting that gave rise to this publication demonstrated a great willingness on the part of the industry to define the terminology, procedures, and eventually the standards needed to enable industrial metrology technology to move ahead as quickly and efficiently as possible. SAE International has demonstrated its lead in this and closely related areas with its Advanced Manufacturing Knowledge Hub on SAE MOBILUS, Advanced Manufacturing Collection, Advanced Manufacturing Standards, and *SAE International Journal of Materials and Manufacturing.*

This SAE EDGE™ Research Report on "Unsettled Technology Domains in Industrial Metrology" identifies the following key topics for further pursuit, both through continued informal discussions among industry practitioners and through more formal working groups:

- **A comprehensive uncertainty framework for industrial measurement** is needed to provide a consistent language and methodology which will enable system-wide considerations of the production system to utilize uncertainty information. Currently different terminology and methods are used for equivalent functions within three methodologies: Metrology, MSA, and SPC.
- **Evaluation of Type B uncertainties** in industrial measurements is required to enable the consideration of effects that haven't been directly observed, such as calibration uncertainty.
- **Evaluating intrinsic uncertainty**: A finite number of discrete measurements, even if the measurements have no uncertainty, leaves uncertainty about the unmeasured regions. There are no established methods of quantifying this uncertainty.
- **Evaluating expected uncertainty of measurement processes:** Current uncertainty evaluation methods only apply to individual measurements after they have been carried out. Manufacturing decisions often require before-the-fact evaluation for processes.
- **Standard industrial uncertainty models**, which allow shared models for instrument and machine elements, and environmental effects will enable complex systems to be readily modeled.
- **Verifying industrial uncertainty models** gives confidence that models are correct.
- **Summarize and extrapolate from MCS** such that complex simulation results can be communicated, and optimization can consider the probability of rare events.
- **Making optimal product verification decisions** involving the selection of instruments, processes, and conformance limits.
- **Making optimal process control decisions** involving the selection of instruments, processes, and conformance limits.

Recommendations

The overall recommendations of this SAE EDGE™ report can be summarized as follows:

1. A unified uncertainty framework will require a standardized vocabulary, suggested here as a subset of the VIM [11], with the addition of concepts of statistical control and conformance limits.
2. A working group should be formed involving technical experts from within both the industry and fundamental metrology research. This group should establish a unified vocabulary, as well as attempt to integrate emerging solutions within the other unresolved domains, discussed below, into a comprehensive uncertainty framework. Doing so will enable system-wide optimization of production systems.
3. Increased awareness is recommended. The fact that MSA can, by omitting Type B sources, significantly underestimate uncertainty needs to be communicated more clearly within the quality engineering community.
4. The issue of how to evaluate expected uncertainty for measurement processes must also be addressed for a model-based approach to be fully adopted. It will then be possible to make valid capability statements which consider effects that cannot be directly observed in gauge study results.
5. Step-by-step procedures supported by readily usable equations, or algorithms, are needed to enable industrial trials of Gaussian processes for the evaluation of intrinsic uncertainty. Trials should then be carried out which validate the assumptions of this approach by comparing predicted surface uncertainties based on a small number of measurement points with high-resolution scanning measurements. This approach should enable the validity of Gaussian processes to be established for specific types of industrial processes. Only at that stage will it be possible to decide whether an alternative approach is required or whether the

suggested approach should be standardized for industrial use.

6. Algorithms able to model intrinsic uncertainty may be used to control intelligent inspection processes. Such an approach could perform an initial rapid inspection and determine whether it gives sufficient confidence to accept or reject. If the intrinsic uncertainty means that neither conformance nor nonconformance can be established, then additional measurement would be automatically carried out. Where quality issues are detected, inspection processes must also ensure that sufficient data has been obtained to support subsequent root cause analysis.
7. A method for the before-the-fact MCS of expected uncertainty has been suggested. Such an approach should be first academically formalized so that uncertainty evaluation can be applied comprehensively to the consideration of uncertainty of measurement and processes within manufacturing. These methods should then undergo industrial trials in order to create robust and practical standards.
8. Significant work is required to compile, develop, and create modular uncertainty models, including instrument and machine elements, environmental effects, datum structures, and intrinsic uncertainty.
9. Algorithms will be required which enable nonstandard distributions and variation in correction values to be propagated through these models. Significant work will be required to create standards that enable complete models to be constructed from the modular components and then run through these algorithms, supporting PUMA. The possibility of using deep learning to construct empirical models from large datasets warrants further investigation, although the significance of Type B evaluation should not be lost in this process.
10. Before an uncertainty framework can be adopted for industrial measurement, robust methods of validating uncertainty models will be required. It will first require a theoretical framework based on experimental design and the methods used in interlaboratory comparisons. Standardized industrial procedures will then be needed, supported by algorithms which enable experimental data to be compared with standard uncertainty models. Tests performed under reduced reproducibility conditions will then provide confidence that the production system will behave as predicted by uncertainty models under the actual conditions of operation.
11. Methods of summarizing probability distributions should be evaluated giving consideration to the requirements of industrial metrology. Highly skewed and high-kurtosis distributions should be used which have been generated by simulation of real industrial measurement and production systems. Using these distributions, methods should be compared in terms of their ability to produce random draws for input into further simulation and efficiently determine CDFs and quantiles at high confidence levels. There should also be some consideration of their ability to provide intuitive communication of the distribution.
12. Compatible methods of evaluating uncertainty in both production and inspection processes are required to minimize the quality-adjusted cost per unit of product sold to the customer. Quality optimization algorithms should be developed, which select production processes and measurement instruments, and set conformance limits to maximize profitability. These novel algorithms will use conditional probabilities, determined from parametric distributions fitted to higher-order moments or cumulants. They will consider costs of production, inspection, and passing defective products to the customer, as well as allow for multiple quality metrics with differing levels of defect resulting in differing quality costs, the cost of reworking, and production delay costs.

Abbreviations/Definitions

After-the-fact uncertainty - The uncertainty of an individual measurement, calculated after the measurement has been made and the values of any corrections made are, therefore, known.

AIAG - Automotive Industry Action Group

ANOVA - (Analysis of variance). A statistical method that allows multiple sources of variation to be identified in a single dataset.

Assignable causes - The term used by Walter A. Shewhart, the father of statistical quality control, to describe systematic effects. These are effects that are not random and may have a known cause.

Before-the-fact uncertainty - An evaluation of the expected uncertainty for a measurement or process which may involve corrections. Because the measurement has not yet been made, the values of any corrections are not yet known, but their variation may be quantified. This is distinct from the uncertainty with which the correction values will be determined at the time of measurement, meaning there are two uncertainties associated with each correction value.

Bias - A consistently repeatable error. More formally expressed as the difference between a reference value and the mean of many repeated measurements.

Chance causes - The term used by Walter A. Shewhart, the father of statistical quality control, to describe random effects.

CMMs - (Coordinate measurement machines). Machines with three linear axes, each with a motor drive and accurate position encoder, which are able to physically probe parts to measure coordinates on their surfaces.

Combined uncertainty - The uncertainty for a measurement, calculated by combining the uncertainties due to each influence quantity.

Common cause - The term used in modern SPC to describe random effects.

Cornish-Fisher expansion - A mathematical approximation which gives specified quantiles from a probability distribution based on its cumulants. It uses an asymptotic expansion. The first four cumulants are the mean, variance, skewness, and kurtosis, respectively, but higher-order expansions also use higher-order cumulants.

Coverage factor - A factor by which a standard uncertainty is multiplied to give increased confidence. This is equivalent to a z-score or sigma level.

Cumulative distribution function - The integral of a probability density function. If this probability distribution is known, this function allows probabilities or confidence intervals to be calculated.

Expected uncertainty - An uncertainty obtained by before-the-fact evaluation of a measurement or process which may involve corrections. Because the measurement has not yet been made, the values of any corrections are not yet known, but their variation may be quantified. This is distinct from the uncertainty with which the correction values will be determined at the time of measurement, meaning there are two uncertainties associated with each correction value.

False decisions - Relates to decisions made on the basis of measurements or test results which have some uncertainty. When the resulting decision is different to what would be decided based on the true value, it is false. For example, a dimension is specified as 10 mm ± 1 mm. A part has a true value of 10.9 mm, but, due to uncertainty in the measurement system, a measurement of 10.11 mm is obtained. This part would be rejected although it actually conforms to the specification, this would, therefore, be a false decision.

Gauge studies - Experiments or tests carried out within MSA to determine the variation of a measurement system. The two main types of gauge study are a *Type 1 gauge study* and a *gauge repeatability and reproducibility (gauge R&R) Study.*

Gaussian - Data or a probability that follows the Gaussian or Normal distribution.

GH distribution - The generalized hyperbolic distribution is a family of continuous probability distributions which includes Student's t, hyperbolic, chi-squared, gamma, and Laplace distributions.

GUM - (Evaluation of measurement data – Guide to the expression of uncertainty in measurement). The definitive document describing the evaluation of uncertainty of measurement, produced by the Joint Committee for Guides in Metrology (JCGM). It has been adopted by all major National Measurement Institutes and standards for testing and calibration laboratories.

Influence quantities - Anything that affects the result of a measurement but which is not the quantity being measured.

Intrinsic uncertainty - The minimum uncertainty possible for a particular object being measured. Even if a measurement system has a negligible uncertainty, uncertainty will remain. For example, due to a finite number of discrete measurement points being unable to fully characterize a continuous surface.

ISO 14253 - This standard deals with "Geometrical product specifications (GPS). Inspection by measurement of workpieces and measuring equipment". Part 2 covers "Guidance for the estimation of uncertainty in GPS measurement, in calibration of measuring equipment and in product verification" which includes a description of the iterative PUMA, a practical method of using worst-case estimates for uncertainties and then obtaining refined estimates only where these have a significant effect.

Kurtosis - The fourth moment of a probability distribution which measures the tails of the distribution. A higher kurtosis indicates more frequent and extreme outliers.

Long-term variability - The variation in a process when the output is observed over a long period of time. This term is typically used within SPC. In other disciplines, the more general term "reproducibility" is normally used.

Markov chain - A mathematical model describing a sequence of events.

MCS - (Monte Carlo simulation). A method of simulating random events using a random number generator. May also be referred to as the Monte Carlo method.

Measurand - The thing being measured.

Metrology - The science of measurement, especially concerned with understanding the uncertainty of measurements. The work and methods of the National Measurement Institutes and accredited calibration laboratories is typically considered to be metrology, differentiating it from the less scientific practices used within some areas of the industry. Within the industry, the term Metrology is also colloquially used to refer to high-quality measurement instruments and their operation.

MPE - (Maximum permissible error). The largest permitted measurement error, with respect to a known reference quantity, as specified for a given measurement, instrument, or measuring system.

MSA - (Measurement systems analysis). A methodology for evaluating the accuracy of measurements using the statistical analysis of repeated measurements. Within the scientific community it has been largely superseded by uncertainty evaluation, with its methods being subsumed within this more rigorous framework. It remains in widespread use within the industry.

MSA Manual - The definitive document describing the use of MSA within manufacturing. It is written by the AIAG.

Pearson distributions - A set of standard types of probability distributions, first defined by Karl Pearson in 1895. The skewness and kurtosis define the type of distribution with the mean and variance also used for fully define a particular distribution. Common probability distributions, such as the Gaussian distribution, may be defined as specific types of Pearson distribution.

Random effects - An effect which results in errors which vary randomly with no apparent cause or pattern.

Random error - An error which results from a random effect.

Repeatability - The closeness of the agreement between the results of successive measurements of the same object, carried out under the same conditions of measurement. The same conditions mean within a small period of time and using the same operator, procedure, instrument, environment, etc.

Reproducibility - The closeness of the agreement between the results of successive measurements of the same object, carried out under changed conditions of measurement. The changed conditions may mean there is a change in the operator, procedure, instrument, environment, etc., or that measurements are carried out over a prolonged period of time.

Short-term variability - The term used within SPC to describe repeatability.

Six Sigma - A process improvement methodology developed at Motorola in the 1980s which prescribes the use of MSA to reduce process variation.

SPC - (Statistical process control). A methodology which uses a set of statistical methods, such as control charts, to monitor and control processes.

Special cause variation - The term used within modern SPC for systematic effects.

Statistical control, stable process - Terms used within SPC for a process in which variation is random and can be characterized by a known probability distribution, typically a Gaussian distribution. This means that there is negligible special cause variation.

Taylor series expansion - A way of a representing a mathematical function as the sum of terms calculated from function's derivatives at a single point. The complete series may be infinite, but expansion to a given order is used as an approximation.

Trueness - The closeness of agreement between the true value and the mean of many measurements.

Tukey's lambda distribution - A continuous and symmetric probability distribution defined in terms of its quantile function.

Type B - A Type B uncertainty evaluation uses any means other than the statistical evaluation of repeated measurements.

Uncertainty evaluation - The process of estimating the uncertainty of a measurement, typically following the principles set out in the GUM.

Uncertainty of measurement - A quantity describing how far a measurement result can be expected to deviate from the true value. It is typically stated as the standard deviation of a probability distribution.

VDA-5 - Capability of Measurement Processes, Capability of Measuring Systems - A standard published by the German Association of the Automotive Industry (Verband Der Automobilindustrie, or VDA), which combines uncertainty evaluation with MSA's gauge studies.

VIM - (International Vocabulary of Metrology). A document produced by the JCGM which attempts to find a common language and terminology in metrology.

Works Cited

1. Airbus, "Financial Statements,"2017.
2. Zhang, X., Xiao, H., Zhang, H., He, X. et al., "Uncertainty Estimation in Form Error Evaluation of Freeform Surfaces for Precision Metrology," in *International Symposium on Precision Mechanical Measurements*, SPIE, Xia'men, China, 2016.
3. Muelaner, J.E., Chappell, M., and Keogh, P.S., "A Unified Approach to Uncertainty for Quality Improvement," in *Laser Metrology and Machine Performance XII*, Renishaw Innovation Centre, UK,2017.
4. JCGM 100: 2008 Evaluation of measurement data – Guide to the expression of uncertainty in measurement.
5. ISO,ISO 3611: 2010 – Geometrical product specifications (GPS) – Dimensional measuring equipment: Micrometers for external measurements - Design and metrological characteristics, 2010 [cited].
6. BSI – British Standards Institution, BS EN ISO 10360-2:2002: 2002 Geometrical Product Specifications (GPS) - Acceptance and reverification tests for coordinate measuring machines (CMM) -Part 2: CMMs used for measuring size.
7. ISO 10360-10: 2016 Geometrical product specifications (GPS) - Acceptance and reverification tests for coordinate measuring systems (CMS) - Laser trackers for measuring point-to-point distances.
8. ISO 2011 ISO 13053-1: Quantitative methods in process improvement - Six Sigma Part 1: DMAIC methodology.
9. Auromotive Industry Action Group, *Measurement Systems Analysis* 4th Edition (2010).

10. ISO 11462-1: 2001 Guidelines for implementation of statistical process control (SPC) - Part 1: Elements of SPC.
11. BSI PD 6461-1: 1995 General Metrology - Part 1: Basic and general terms (VIM).
12. ISO, "5725: Accuracy (trueness and precision) of measurement methods and results," Part 1: General principles and definitions 1994 [cited].
13. Shewhart, W.A., *Economic Control of Quality of Manufactured Product* (New York: Van Nostrand, 1931).
14. Forbes, A. and Perruchet, C., *Measurement Systems Analysis: Concepts and Computational Approaches* (Rio de Janeiro, Brazil: IMEKO-International Measurement Federation Secretariat, 2006).
15. Muelaner, J.E., Francis, A.J., Chappell, M., and Maropoulos, P.G., "A Hybrid Measurement Systems Analysis and Uncertainty of Measurement Approach for Industrial Measurement in the Light Controlled Factory," in *Second International Conference on Sustainable Design and Manufacturing*, Seville, Spain, 2015, www.muelaner.com/quality-assurance/hybrid-msa-and-uncertainty/.
16. BSI PD 6461-3: 1995 General Metrology - Part 3: Guide to the expression of uncertainty in measurement (GUM).
17. ISO 14253-2: 2011 Geometrical product specifications (GPS). Inspection by measurement of workpieces and measuring equipment. Guidance for the estimation of uncertainty in GPS measurement, in calibration of measuring equipment and in product verification.
18. German Association of the Automotive Industry, "Capability of Measurement Processes, Capability of Measuring Systems – Test process suitability, suitability of measuring systems, measurement and test processes, extended measurement uncertainty, conformity assessment," VDA-5, 2nd edn., 2011 [cited].
19. Joint Committee for Guides in Metrology, "Evaluation of measurement data – Supplement 1 to the 'Guide to the expression of uncertainty in measurement' - Propagation of distributions using a Monte Carlo method," 2007.
20. BSI, BS EN ISO 1101: 2005 Geometrical Product Specifications (GPS) – Geometrical tolerancing - Tolerances of form, orientation, location and run-out.
21. ASME Y14.5-2018: 2018 Dimensioning and Tolerancing.
22. Forbes, A.B., "Uncertainty Associated with Form Assessment in Coordinate Metrology," *International Journal of Metrology and Quality Engineering* 4(1):17-22, 2013, doi:10.1051/ijmqe/2012032.
23. Muelaner, J.E., Ross-Pinnock, D., Mullineux, G., and Keogh, P.S., "Uncertainties in Dimensional Measurements due to Thermal Expansion," in *Laser Metrology and Machine Performance XII*, Renishaw Innovation Centre, Gloucestershire, 2017.
24. Forbes, A.B., "Measurement Uncertainty and Optimized Conformance Assessment," *Measurement* 39:808-814, 2006.
25. Pendrill, L.R., "Optimised Measurement Uncertainty and Decision-Making in Conformity Assessment," *NCSLi Measure* 2(2):76-86, 2007.
26. Hughes, B., Forbes, A., Lewis, A., Sun, W. et al., "Laser Tracker Error Determination Using a Network Measurement," *Measurement Science and Technology* 22:1-12, 2011.
27. Muelaner, J.E., Wadsworth, W., Azini, M., Mullineux, G. et al., "Absolute Multilateration between Spheres," *Meas. Sci. Technol.* 28(4):045005, 2017.
28. Flynna, J.M., Muelanera, J.E., Dhokiaa, V., and Newman, S.T., "Improving Error Models of Machine Tools with Metrology Data," *Procedia CIRP* 52:204-209, 2016.
29. Jagan, K. and Forbes, A.B., "Assessing Interlaboratory Comparison Data Adjustment Procedures," *International Journal of Metrology and Quality Engineering* 10:1-8, 2019, doi:10.1051/ijmqe/2019003.
30. Ferrero, C., "The Equivalence in Accreditation: Robust or Standard Statistical Analysis of Interlaboratory Comparisons," *Measurement: Journal of the International Measurement Confederation* 42(10):1541-1545, 2009, doi:10.1016/j.measurement.2009.07.011.
31. Huang, H., "A New Method for Estimating Consensus Values in Interlaboratory Comparisons," *Metrologia* 55(1):106-113, 2018, doi:10.1088/1681-7575/aaa170.
32. Koepke, A., Lafarge, T., Possolo, A., and Toman, B., "Consensus Building for Interlaboratory Studies, Key Comparisons, and Meta-Analysis," *Metrologia* 54(3):S34-S62, 2017, doi:10.1088/1681-7575/aa6c0e.
33. Muelaner, J.E., Wang, Z., Keogh, P.S., Brownell, J. et al., "Uncertainty of Measurement for Large Product Verification: Evaluation of a Large Aero Gas Turbine Engine," *Meas. Sci. Technol.* 27(11):12, 2016.
34. Sim, C.H. and Lim, M.H., "Evaluating Expanded Uncertainty in Measurement with a Fitted Distribution," *Metrologia* 45:178-284, 2008.
35. Harris, P.M., Matthews, C.E., Cox, M.G., and Forbes, A.B., "Summarizing the Output of a Monte Carlo Method for Uncertainty Evaluation," *Metrologia* 51(3):243-252, 2014, doi:10.1088/0026-1394/51/3/243.
36. Anderson, T.V. and Matterson, C.A., "Propagating Skewness and Kurtosis through Engineering Models for Low-Cost, Meaningful, Nondeterministic Design," *Journal of Mechanical Design* 134(10):100911, 2012.
37. Song, T., Wang, S., and An, W., *GPS Positioning Accuracy Estimation Using Cornish-Fisher*

Expansion (Kunming, China: IEEE Computer Society, 2009).

38. Rajan, A., Kuang, Y.C., Ooi, M.P.-L., and Demidenko, S.N., "Benchmark Test Distributions for Expanded Uncertainty Evaluation Algorithms," *IEEE Transactions on Instrumentation and Measurement* 65(5):1022-1034, 2016, doi:10.1109/tim.2015.2507418.
39. Lee, S.H. and Chen, W., "A Comparative Study of Uncertainty Propagation Methods for Black-Box-Type Problems," *Structural and Multidisciplinary Optimization* 37(3):239-253, 2009, doi:10.1007/s00158-008-0234-7.
40. BSI, BS EN ISO 14253-1:1999: 1999 Geometrical Product Specifications (GPS) - Inspection by Measurement of Workpieces and Measuring Equipment - Part 1: Decision Rules for Proving Conformance or Non-Conformance with Specifications.
41. Pendrill, L.R., "Optimised Uncertainty and Cost Operating Characteristics: New Tools for Conformity Assessment. Application to Geometrical Product Control in Automobile Industry," *Int. J. Metrol. Qual. Eng.* 1:105-110, 2010.
42. Pendrill, L.R., "Using Measurement Uncertainty in Decision-Making and Conformity Assessment," *Metrologia* 51:207-219, 2014.

Contact Information

EDGEresearch@sae.org.

The authors of this document together with the SAE Team responsible for its creation join in expressing our deepest appreciation to all of the individuals who contributed.